THE GRAND INQUISITOR
ON THE NATURE OF MAN

The Library of Liberal Arts

Fyodor Dostoevski

THE GRAND INQUISITOR ON THE NATURE OF MAN

FYODOR DOSTOEVSKI

Translated by
CONSTANCE GARNETT
with an introduction by
WILLIAM HUBBEN

WOOD ENGRAVINGS BY FRITZ EICHENBERG
· ·
The Library of Liberal Arts

Macmillan Publishing Company
New York
Collier Macmillan Publishers
London

Fyodor Dostoevski: 1821-1881

THE BROTHERS KARAMAZOV was originally published in 1880

• • • • • • • • • • • • • • • • • • •

Macmillan Publishing Company
866 Third Avenue
New York, New York 10022

First Edition
Twenty-fifth Printing — 1987

ISBN: 0-02-340600-3

INTRODUCTION

Fyodor M. Dostoevski (1821-1881) went through a great many trying experiences and inward changes that seemed to predestine him for the writing of his final masterpiece *The Brothers Karamazov.* His childhood and adolescence introduced him early to the sordid side of life and already in his younger years he took refuge from life in a vast amount of reading. After an initial success as a free-lance writer, he was arrested for activities in a socialist group and sentenced to death. A few minutes before his execution was to take place, the Czar's reprieve was read to him and his fellow prisoners and he was banished to Siberia where he spent long years in the company of the most abject and unhappy prisoners. After his release, there followed an erratic life of trial and error in journalistic enterprises, passionate and turbulent love affairs, a chaotic search for happiness in gambling, and an Odyssey of roving over the European continent. Many of the characters of his novels are men and women with twisted minds, some plainly abnormal, others oscillating between saintliness and license, and the poor, the despised, the misunderstood and unhappy have hardly ever been portrayed by other writers with as much insight and sympathy as by Dostoevski in his short stories and novels. His own physical torments (he was epileptic), his burning love for life, and the never-ending haste, to which his debts and the pressure of merciless publishers forced him, could not prevent him from rallying at the end of his life to the supreme effort of writing *The Brothers Karamazov* of which he had dreamed for years. It was to be the book in which "everything will be said" and it rounded out the preceding works *Crime and Punishment, The Idiot,* and *The Possessed* to one vast panorama of man's eternal homesickness for spiritual values. It may be said of

Dostoevski that he traveled the infinite orbit between heaven and hell with as much consciousness as rarely another poet and dramatist before and after him. His place will always be among the greatest in world literature.

The Brothers Karamazov, from which *The Grand Inquisitor* is taken, tells the story of a family tragedy. The father is a man of many passions and weaknesses and full of vehement, animal vitality. Now and then he shows a surprisingly deep insight into human nature while remaining an eruptive, incalculable and utterly selfish cynic. His four sons suffer from various splits in their personalities. Alyosha, cast in the mold of sainthood, suggests at times that he too is secretly fragile. He is a churchman and lives in the mysteries of the invisible but has not yet attained the "unmixed wisdom" of the pure. Dmitri is impulsive and can be as chaotic as his father but lives, generally, on a higher level than his parent. Smerdyakov, the illegitimate degenerate, kills his father in the final tragedy in which money, lust, jealousy and the most primitive instincts make a weird mesh of guilt and fate.

Ivan represents the intellectual element in this family gallery. In many respects he is the double of several other characters in Dostoevski's novels and—of Dostoevski himself. Full of zest for living, he too is a divided man. He wavers between intellectual honesty and a moral nihilism that is as arrogant as that of the murderer Raskolnikov in *Crime and Punishment* and it is no surprise that his incessant play with truth and its perversions brings him close to insanity. But he has our sympathy when he rebels against society and a church which deny social justice to the many sufferers of his time. He is an atheist, yet he is also compelled to admit the existence of God, or at least of a God of his own making: if man is responsible to God, so he argues, God is also responsible to man, and it is therefore only logical that he quarrels with Him about senseless suffering and injustice in human life. Traits such as these were part of Dostoevski's own development and experience.

Suffering is the theme of *The Grand Inquisitor* which Ivan undertook to write and read to his brother Alyosha. It carries the elemental force of a vision and raises Ivan, at least for a moment, to the realm of prophetic poetry. But this scene is not the only key to Ivan's character. He reveals himself equally strongly in another scene of the novel which is quite different because of its hallucinatory nature. The reader of *The Grand Inquisitor* should compare it with Ivan's nightmarish dialogue toward the end of the novel with the devil who mockingly calls him his "poor relation" and whose cunning reveals him at once as a close sibling of the infernal Screwtape and Wormwood tribe in which our generation, for obvious reasons, has again become so keenly interested. To suggest the reading of this scene implies, of course, the reading of the entire novel. *The Grand Inquisitor* alone cannot convey the grandiose and dark beauty of the full novel and its message.

The Grand Inquisitor stands high above all similar attempts of our poets, dramatists, and novelists to deal with the figure of Christ. All such portraits in American and European literature are done on too small a canvas and with faded colors.

Dostoevski's story rises from a moment of apostolic illumination. There is nothing experimental about it. It has the reality and majesty of an apparition and recalls at once the Biblical moment in which Pontius Pilate directs his defiant remark to the prisoner that Truth means nothing in this world of power politics, court intrigue, and finances. Such a comparison with the Gospel is quite in order, notwithstanding our reverence for the Bible. Like the Grand Inquisitor, Pilate does not really expect an answer when asking a question. Both Pilate and the Inquisitor are of the kind who know all the answers and dress them in the cynical lingo of a query. This is not to construe a forced identity of Pilate with the Grand Inquisitor. The cardinal's motives for his actions differ greatly from Pilate's. But the spiritual kinship of the two is obvious. *The Grand Inquisitor* should be part of a Fifth Gospel if we might ever compose such a piece containing our most magnificent creations including the best thoughts of mankind on Jesus.

There are, as one would expect, some paradoxes in the setting which brings Jesus and the cardinal together. Christ comes not to inspect the Church or condemn society as He was made to do in Sinclair's *They Call Me Carpenter*. He never came to condemn nor did He need to inspect our institutions. Ivan, the atheist, says, "In His infinite mercy He deigned to come down to His servants." But condemnation is there all the same: the cardinal, the Church in person, condemns Him and thereby condemns his Church. The returning Jesus may have wanted to visit the Church that professes love while burning the heretics and thus practices hate. But He had no time to proceed from its steps inside. The Church lays its heavy hand upon Him after the poor and humble have recognized Him at once. And when the cardinal lets his volcanic rage pour over his prisoner, Christ never replies. As Nicholas Berdyaev points out, it is noteworthy that "the extremely powerful vindication of Christ . . . should be put into the mouth of the atheist Ivan Karamazov. It is indeed a puzzle, and it is not clear on the face of it which side the speaker is on, and on which side the writer; we are left free to interpret and understand for ourselves: that which deals with liberty is addressed to the free."

That is, of course, as it ought to be. All truly significant thoughts are clothed in silence. Those abysmal desires that mattered in the later conversations between Smerdyakov and Ivan and led to the terrible consequences of murder remained also unspoken but they were well understood by both. Truth and Vision are likewise beyond words. "Efficacious religion does not explain itself, the principle of freedom cannot be expressed in words; but the principle of compulsion (the cardinal) puts its case very freely indeed," says Berdyaev, and the final Truth emerges from the Inquisitor's own contradictions, whereas only Christ's silence speaks convincingly.

Another paradox is inherent in the nature of Christian faith. The Grand Inquisitor speaks for the centuries when he characterizes man as weak, shortsighted, cowardly, and even wild and vicious. Christianity, to him, is not a matter for the millions. He thinks that only a few are capable of rising above the masses and comprehending the spirituality of Jesus' teachings and life. In this, he anticipates merely our own evasions ("His standards are simply too high. It can't be done"), not realizing that an ideal ceases to exist when we reduce it to the "possible." The cardinal's is a harsh verdict. Yet it is only on the surface a judgment of impatience and angry boredom. He believes in being realistic. But this realism is no new discovery. There have been at all times those who would not take their chances with freedom and love. They prefer to see life "as it is," not as it ought to be. Realists of his kind are apt to ignore the reality of the Spirit.

But the cardinal does not stop here. There are deeper mainsprings in him: he cares for the people. He suffers from the burden of leadership and it is not fair to condemn him as impulsively as we reject the Caesars, Borgias, and Hitlers. He suffers from the very deception he has to practice. "We shall be forced to lie," and "we have corrected Thy work," he says to Jesus, and there is something grotesque in the cardinal's eagerness to persuade his august prisoner. He talks as though Christ had overlooked the most obvious traits of man and thereby discloses that he himself has yet to comprehend the elements of Christian faith which are love and the freedom of choice between good and evil. That these are qualitative states of the mind and not a matter of statistics has not yet occurred to him.

His appalling secret is, of course, that he does not believe in God, as Alyosha exclaims after having listened to the story. He can, *therefore,* not believe in man. Faith and worship, like love and freedom, have their sole origin in God. The cardinal passes on from man's ineradicable desire to worship (our generation calls it "incurable") to pointing at schisms and religious wars as proof of Christ's failure. He knows the solution, the way toward unity for mankind. It is the abolition of hunger and misery, or "the banner of earthly bread." Such wisdom is clearly that of an earthly ruler: the cardinal is not the prince of the Church he is meant to be.

The scene is laid in Spain, four hundred years ago, but we ought to guard against reading it as a piece of European history. The problem of Freedom versus Compulsion is facing us in our personal and corporate life with real urgency, though not yet so dramatically as it arose abroad. The choice between good and evil cannot, and must not, be spared any one of us.

It is only natural that this story discusses freedom and compulsion in terms of the Church and of faith, whereas we think of them as a predominantly political and personal matter. The recent breakdown of liberty in the life of most European nations is regarded by many of us as a threat to democracy all over the world. Prosperity, free enterprise, and democracy are endangered. We, too, wonder whether state interference and regulation of trade and commerce, even in a mild degree, may not become a real menace to our hard-won liberties and ultimately extend to matters of political and religious freedom. The story of the Inquisitor is set in an age that knew nothing of the separation of Church and State. We shall, therefore, have to translate much of the story into secular terms to see its implications for modern times.

Evil, social injustice, suffering, and sin are conditions of man's inner freedom, hard to win and even harder to endure. Our time has witnessed human catastrophes such as were unknown to Dostoevski. Each one was <u>preceded by</u> <u>religious decay,</u> <u>scientific optimism,</u> and a <u>delight in tech-</u><u>nological "realism"</u> which acknowledged all of the novel-ist's prophecies. A <u>decade after</u> Dostoevski's death in 1881, we read how <u>Nietzsche's</u> superman started out to teach his fateful heresy of the "<u>much-too-many,</u>" the despised mob, to be ruled by the superman who was his own law to him-self. His Zarathustra elevated himself beyond good and evil to attain a higher vision, and before Zarathustra began to teach he remarked rather casually that God had died. Zara-thustra, then, was a close relative of Ivan, Raskolnikov, Stavrogin, and the Grand Inquisitor, and it appears sig-nificant when Nietzsche could say that Dostoevski was "the only psychologist from whom I had anything to learn." Now we know that the proud discovery of God's death was noth-ing more than the beginning of our present fear. We are wondering whether mankind will be able to survive.

André Gide counts Dostoevski among the great incen-diaries of the soul and the time is rapidly drawing to a close when he could regret that the enormous shadow of Tolstoi was obscuring our vision of the mission of Russian litera-ture to the West. Both Tolstoi and Dostoevski wrestled with the spirit of Christ in their way. Tolstoi's angry writ-ings on theology were a courageous frontal attack against church and society but they never reached the millions at home and abroad as effectually as his masterful novels in which religious accords are rare and feeble. His characters seem to flee into the realm of religion mainly when they suffer and feel lost in the wilderness of their hearts. In this, they reflect Tolstoi's own dilemma, as an aristocrat who tried in vain to be an amateur peasant and a lusty pantheist who longed to be a primitive, an "early" Christian. Tolstoi, too, knows of a way to create happiness. But his solution re-sembles closely that of the shallow claim of his German contemporaries who called Jesus "the first socialist." Merely to divide and distribute man's property will never heal the pains of his soul and conscience. The morale of a group of socialists may be admirable, but it can never match the spirit of the early Christians.

A generation before Dostoevski's *The Brothers Karamazov* was written, Kierkegaard accused the Christian Church of having lost its mission. Christianity, to him, was a shocking optical illusion without any real spiritual existence. His indignant cries against bishops, pastors, and Sunday Christians were sincere, but compared with the Grand Inquisitor his voice appears now desperate and perhaps also a bit hysterical. The present story leads us into a distinctly different climate of thought: the Grand Inquisitor declares, with sinister poise, to the very face of Christ that he must work against Him—not with Him. He drops all pretenses.

Such are some of the underlying implications of *The Grand Inquisitor*. Our generation, schooled in the psychology of man's dualisms, will read it with new eyes. The Inquisitor's disdain for the average man was amply vindicated in the totalitarian movements abroad which were not, in their inception, a matter of brutal suppression of the millions by a few self-styled supermen. These millions of misguided men and women (although not the entire nations) enthroned them freely with jubilation and then "laid their freedom at their feet," precisely as the Inquisitor had prophesied. They were as tired of insecurity and feeble democratic experiments as their democratic leaders. But we may well believe that the ultimate judgment of history will be more severe with the leaders than with their followers.

One may do wrong by applying this scene also to socialism, as Berdyaev does, to political events, or only to Catholicism of which Dostoevski had no profound knowledge. An image as panoramic and fervent as this tale lends itself to a variety of interpretations and a bias is almost unavoidable when we try to fathom its meaning. Dostoevski never went into pamphleteering. His novels explore man's soul and his characters produce the plots as logically as our own virtues and passions weave the patterns of our lives. Both characters and action were born from the writer's torments of doubt and suffering and will always intensify light and darkness in the reader. He does not intend to give answers but wants us to ask better questions. Those longing for freedom will have to do more than accept solutions, follow orders, or assent to proof. That may be the key to the strange ending of this scene which has been called inconclusive. We must remember that we have witnessed Truth and its eloquent counterpart. The latter took his arguments from the stores of our racial memory and ignored the homesickness of man's soul. But we feel that there is a noble fulfillment answering our God-given sense of expectancy because of the existence of Truth in Christ. The quest for Truth leads into uncharted regions, beautiful and hazardous.

The reader will feel an obligation to acquaint himself with Dostoevski's life and work after the reading of *The Grand Inquisitor*. An adequate appreciation of either would go far beyond the small compass of this essay. We recommend Janko Lavrin's *Dostoevsky, a Study* (Macmillan) as a well-informed and, within its short space, a sound presentation. J. A. T. Lloyd's *Fyodor Dostoevsky* (Scribner's) addresses itself to those who are familiar with the cultural history of Western and Central Europe and are chiefly interested in the literary element. Ernest J. Simmons' *Dostoevski, the Making of a Novelist* (Oxford) also analyzes the novelist's development as a writer without attempting a satisfying philosophical approach. Nicholas Berdyaev's *Dostoevsky* (Sheed & Ward) is the profoundest religious study in the field but demands of the reader a good deal of patience before granting its rich rewards. André Gide's *Dostoevsky* (Knopf) is still one of the most appreciative and lucid interpretations. It was written almost a generation ago and republished in 1946, in France. Perhaps I may be permitted to add to this list the essay on Dostoevski in my book *Four Prophets of Our Destiny* (Macmillan). It attempts to appraise him within the context of the thinking of Kierkegaard, Nietzsche, and Kafka, as well as a religiously oriented existentialism.

WILLIAM HUBBEN

NOTE ON THE TEXT

The Grand Inquisitor is Chapter V in Book V of Fyodor Dostoevski's last novel *The Brothers Karamazov,* written in 1880. The translation from the Russian is by Constance Garnett, as published in Volume I, *The Novels of Fyodor Dostoevsky,* and is used by permission of The Macmillan Company, publishers.

Fritz Eichenberg has prepared the wood engravings for this edition, one portraying the author and the other setting forth the main theme of the story with great eloquence. He has also engraved the decoration used on the half-title page.

The present edition follows, with minor changes, the edition published by the Association Press, New York, New York, and is here issued by permission of The Edward W. Hazen Foundation, New Haven, Conn.

O.P.

THE GRAND INQUISITOR
ON THE NATURE OF MAN

"   . . . Do you know, Alyosha—don't laugh! I made a poem about a year ago. If you can waste another ten minutes on me, I'll tell it to you."

"You wrote a poem?"

"Oh, no, I didn't write it," laughed Ivan, "and I've never written two lines of poetry in my life. But I made up this poem in prose and I remembered it. I was carried away when I made it up. You will be my first reader—that is, listener. Why should an author forego even one listener?" smiled Ivan. "Shall I tell it to you?"

"I am all attention," said Alyosha.

"My poem is called 'The Grand Inquisitor'; it's a ridiculous thing, but I want to tell it to you."

"EVEN THIS MUST HAVE A PREFACE—THAT IS, A LITERARY preface," laughed Ivan, "and I am a poor hand at making one. You see, my action takes place in the sixteenth century, and at that time, as you probably learnt at school, it was customary in poetry to bring down heavenly powers on earth. Not to speak of Dante, in France clerks, as well as the monks in the monasteries, used to give regular performances in which the Madonna, the saints, the angels, Christ, and God Himself were brought on the stage. In those days it was done in all simplicity. In Victor Hugo's 'Notre Dame de Paris' an edifying and gratuitous spectacle was provided for the people in the Hotel de Ville of Paris in the reign of Louis XI in honor of the birth of the dauphin. It was called *Le bon jugement de la très sainte et gracieuse Vierge Marie,* and she appears herself on the stage and pronounces her *bon jugement.* Similar plays, chiefly from the Old Testament, were occasionally performed in Moscow, too, up to the times of Peter the Great. But besides plays there were all sorts of legends and ballads scattered about the world, in which the saints and angels and all the powers of Heaven took part when required. In our monasteries the monks busied themselves in translating, copying, and even composing such poems— and even under the Tatars. There is, for instance, one such poem (of course, from the Greek), 'The Wanderings of Our Lady Through Hell,' with descriptions as bold as Dante's. Our Lady visits Hell, and the Archangel Michael leads her through the torments. She sees the sinners and their punishment. There she sees among others one noteworthy set of sinners in a burning lake; some of them sink to the bottom of the lake so that they can't swim out, and 'these God forgets'—an expression of extraordinary depth and force. And so Our Lady, shocked and weeping, falls before the throne of God and begs for mercy for all in Hell—for all she has seen there, and indiscriminately. Her conversation with God is immensely interesting. She beseeches Him, she will not desist, and when God points to the hands and feet of her Son, nailed to the Cross, and asks, 'How can I forgive His tormentors?' she bids all the saints, all the martyrs, all the angels and archangels to fall down with her and pray for mercy on all without distinction. It ends by her winning from God a respite of suffering every year from Good Friday till Trinity day, and the sinners at once raise a cry of thankfulness from Hell, chanting, 'Thou art just, O Lord, in this judgment.' Well, my poem would have been of that kind if it had appeared at that time. He comes on the scene in my poem, but He says nothing, only appears and passes on. Fifteen centuries have passed since He promised to come in His glory, fifteen centuries since His prophet wrote, 'Behold, I come quickly'; 'Of that day and that hour knoweth no man, neither the Son, but the Father,' as He Himself predicted on earth. But humanity awaits him with the same faith and with the same love. Oh, with greater faith, for it is fifteen centuries since man has ceased to see signs from Heaven.

> No signs from Heaven come today
> To add to what the heart doth say.

There was nothing left but faith in what the heart doth say. It is true there were many miracles in those days. There were saints who performed miraculous cures; some holy people, according to their biographies, were visited by the Queen of Heaven herself. But the devil did not slumber, and doubts were already arising among men of the truth of these miracles. And just then there appeared in the north of Germany a terrible new heresy. 'A huge star like to a torch' (that is, to a church) 'fell on the sources of the waters and they became bitter.' These heretics began blasphemously denying miracles. But those who remained faithful were all the more ardent in their faith. The tears of humanity rose up to Him as before, awaiting His coming, loved Him, hoped for Him, yearned to suffer and die for Him as before. And so many ages mankind had prayed with faith and fervor, 'O Lord our God, hasten Thy coming,' so many ages called upon Him, that in His infinite mercy He deigned to come down to His servants. Before that day He had come down, He had visited some holy men, martyrs, and hermits, as is written in their 'Lives.' Among us, Tyutchev, with absolute faith in the truth of his words, bore witness that

Bearing the Cross, in slavish dress,
Weary and worn, the Heavenly King
Our mother, Russia, came to bless,
And through our land went wandering.

And that certainly was so, I assure you.

"And behold, He deigned to appear for a moment to the people, to the tortured, suffering people, sunk in iniquity, but loving Him like children. My story is laid in Spain, in Seville, in the most terrible time of the Inquisition, when fires were lighted every day to the glory of God, and 'in the splendid *auto da fé* the wicked heretics were burnt.' Oh, of course, this was not the coming in which He will appear according to His promise at the end of time in all His heavenly glory, and which will be sudden 'as lightning flashing from east to west.' No, He visited His children only for a moment, and there where the flames were crackling round the heretics. In His infinite mercy He came once more among men in that human shape in which He walked among men for three years fifteen centuries ago. He came down to the 'hot pavement' of the southern town in which on the day before almost a hundred heretics had, *ad majorem gloriam Dei,* been burnt by the cardinal, the Grand Inquisitor, in a magnificent *auto da fé,* in the presence of the king, the court, the knights, the cardinals, the most charming ladies of the court, and the whole population of Seville.

"He came softly, unobserved, and yet, strange to say, every one recognized Him. That might be one of the best passages in the poem. I mean, why they recognized Him. The people are irresistibly drawn to Him, they surround Him. they flock about Him, follow Him. He

moves silently in their midst with a gentle smile of infinite compassion. The sun of love burns in His heart,
light and power shine from His eyes, and their radiance,
shed on the people, stirs their hearts with responsive
love. He holds out His hands to them, blesses them, and
a healing virtue comes from contact with Him, even
with His garments. An old man in the crowd, blind
from childhood, cries out, 'O Lord, heal me and I shall
see Thee!' and, as it were, scales fall from his eyes and
the blind man sees Him. The crowd weeps and kisses
the earth under His feet. Children throw flowers before
Him, sing, and cry hosannah. 'It is He—it is He!' all repeat. 'It must be He, it can be no one but Him!' He
stops at the steps of the Seville cathedral at the moment
when the weeping mourners are bringing in a little open
white coffin. In it lies a child of seven, the only daughter
of a prominent citizen. The dead child lies hidden in
flowers. 'He will raise your child,' the crowd shouts to
the weeping mother. The priest, coming to meet the
coffin, looks perplexed and frowns, but the mother of
the dead child throws herself at His feet with a wail. 'If
it is Thou, raise my child!' she cries, holding out her
hands to Him. The procession halts, the coffin is laid on
the steps at His feet. He looks with compassion, and His
lips once more softly pronounce, 'Maiden, arise!' and
the maiden arises. The little girl sits up in the coffin
and looks round, smiling with wide-open wondering
eyes, holding a bunch of white roses they had put in her
hand.

"There are cries, sobs, confusion among the people,
and at that moment the cardinal himself, the Grand
Inquisitor, passes by the cathedral. He is an old man,
almost ninety, tall and erect, with a withered face and

sunken eyes, in which there is still a gleam of light. He
is not dressed in his gorgeous cardinal's robes, as he was
the day before, when he was burning the enemies of
the Roman Church—at that moment he was wearing his
coarse, old, monk's cassock. At a distance behind him
come his gloomy assistants and slaves and the 'holy
guard.' He stops at the sight of the crowd and watches
it from a distance. He sees everything; he sees them set
the coffin down at His feet, sees the child rise up, and his
face darkens. He knits his thick grey brows and his eyes
gleam with a sinister fire. He holds out his finger and
bids the guards take Him. And such is his power, so
completely are the people cowed into submission and
trembling obedience to him, that the crowd immedi-
ately makes way for the guards, and in the midst of
deathlike silence they lay hands on Him and lead Him
away. The crowd instantly bows down to the earth, like
one man, before the old inquisitor. He blesses the people in silence and passes on. The guards lead their
prisoner to the close, gloomy, vaulted prison in the ancient palace of the Holy Inquisition and shut Him in
it. The day passes and is followed by the dark, burning
'breathless' night of Seville. The air is 'fragrant with
laurel and lemon.' In the pitch darkness the iron door
of the prison is suddenly opened and the Grand Inquisitor himself comes in with a light in his hand. He is
alone; the door is closed at once behind him. He stands
in the doorway and for a minute or two gazes into His
face. At last he goes up slowly, sets the light on the
table and speaks.

" 'Is it Thou? Thou?' but receiving no answer, he
adds at once, 'Don't answer, be silent. What canst Thou
say, indeed? I know too well what Thou wouldst say.

And Thou hast no right to add anything to what Thou hadst said of old. Why, then, art Thou come to hinder us? For Thou hast come to hinder us, and Thou knowest that. But dost Thou know what will be tomorrow? I know not who Thou art and care not to know whether it is Thou or only a semblance of Him, but tomorrow I shall condemn Thee and burn Thee at the stake as the worst of heretics. And the very people who have today kissed Thy feet, tomorrow at the faintest sign from me will rush to heap up the embers of Thy fire. Knowest Thou that? Yes, maybe Thou knowest it,' he added with thoughtful penetration, never for a moment taking his eyes off the Prisoner."

"I don't quite understand, Ivan. What does it mean?" Alyosha, who had been listening in silence, said with a smile. "Is it simply a wild fantasy, or a mistake on the part of the old man—some impossible *qui pro quo?*"

"Take it as the last," said Ivan, laughing, "if you are so corrupted by modern realism and can't stand anything fantastic. If you like it to be a case of mistaken identity, let it be so. It is true," he went on, laughing, "the old man was ninety, and he might well be crazy over his set idea. He might have been struck by the appearance of the Prisoner. It might, in fact, be simply his ravings, the delusion of an old man of ninety, overexcited by the *auto da fé of* a hundred heretics the day before. But does it matter to us after all whether it was a mistake of identity or a wild fantasy? All that matters is that the old man should speak out, should speak openly of what he has thought in silence for ninety years."

"And the Prisoner too is silent? Does He look at him and not say a word?"

"That's inevitable in any case," Ivan laughed again.
"The old man has told Him He hasn't the right to add
anything to what He has said of old. One may say it
is the most fundamental feature of Roman Catholicism,
in my opinion at least. 'All has been given by Thee to
the Pope,' they say, 'and all, therefore, is still in the
Pope's hands, and there is no need for Thee to come
now at all. Thou must not meddle for the time, at least.'
That's how they speak and write, too—the Jesuits, at any
rate. I have read it myself in the works of their the-
ologians. 'Hast Thou the right to reveal to us one of
the mysteries of that world from which Thou hast
come?' my old man asks Him, and answers the question
for Him. 'No, Thou has not; that Thou mayest not add
to what has been said of old, and mayest not take from
men the freedom which Thou didst exalt when Thou
wast on earth. Whatsoever Thou revealest anew will
encroach on men's freedom of faith; for it will be mani-
fest as a miracle, and the freedom of their faith was
dearer to Thee than anything in those days fifteen hundred years ago. Didst Thou not often say then, "I will
make you free"? But now Thou hast seen these "free"
men,' the old man adds suddenly, with a pensive smile.
'Yes, we've paid dearly for it,' he goes on, looking sternly
at Him, 'but at last we have completed that work in
Thy name. For fifteen centuries we have been wrestling
with Thy freedom, but now it is ended and over for
good. Dost Thou not believe that it's over for good?
Thou lookest meekly at me and deignest not even to
be wroth with me. But let me tell Thee that now, today, people are more persuaded than ever that they have
perfect freedom, yet they have brought their freedom to
us and laid it humbly at our feet. But that has been

our doing. Was this what Thou didst? Was this Thy freedom?' "

"I don't understand again," Alyosha broke in. "Is he ironical, is he jesting?"

"Not a bit of it! He claims it as a merit for himself and his Church that at last they have vanquished freedom and have done so to make men happy. 'For now' (he is speaking of the Inquisition, of course) 'for the first time it has become possible to think of the happiness of men. Man was created a rebel; and how can rebels be happy? Thou wast warned,' he says to Him. 'Thou hast had no lack of admonitions, and warnings, but Thou didst not listen to those warnings; Thou didst reject the only way by which men might be made happy. But, fortunately, departing Thou didst hand on the work to us. Thou hast promised, Thou hast established by Thy word, Thou hast given to us the right to bind and to unbind, and now, of course, Thou canst not think of taking it away. Why, then, hast Thou come to hinder us?' "

"And what's the meaning of 'no lack of admonitions and warnings'?" asked Alyosha.

"Why, that's the chief part of what the old man must say.

" 'The wise and dread Spirit, the spirit of self-destruction and nonexistence,' the old man goes on, 'the great spirit talked with Thee in the wilderness, and we are told in the books that he "tempted" Thee. Is that so? And could anything truer be said than what he revealed to Thee in three questions and what Thou didst reject, and what in the books is called "the temptation"? And yet if there has ever been on earth a real stupendous miracle, it took place on that day, on the day of the three temptations. The statement of those three questions was itself the miracle. If it were possible to imagine simply for the sake of argument that those three questions of the dread spirit had perished utterly from the books, and that we had to restore them and to invent them anew, and to do so had gathered together all the wise men of the earth—rulers, chief priests, learned men, philosophers, poets—and had set them the task to invent three questions, such as would not only fit the occasion, but express in three words, three human phrases, the whole future history of the world and of humanity—dost Thou believe that all the wisdom of the earth united could have invented anything in depth and force equal to the three questions which were actually put to Thee then by the wise and mighty spirit in the wilderness? From those questions alone, from the miracle of their statement, we can see that we have here to do not with the fleeting human intelligence, but with the absolute and eternal. For in those three questions the whole subsequent history of mankind is, as it were, brought together into one whole, and foretold, and in them are united all the unsolved historical contradictions of human nature. At the time it could not be so clear, since the future was unknown; but now that fifteen hundred years have passed, we see that everything in those three questions was so justly divined and foretold, and has been so truly fulfilled, that nothing can be added to them or taken from them.

" 'Judge Thyself who was right—Thou or he who questioned Thee then? Remember the first question; its meaning, in other words, was this: "Thou wouldst go into the world, and art going with empty hands, with some promise of freedom which men in their simplicity and their natural unruliness cannot even understand, which they fear and dread—for nothing has ever been more insupportable for a man and a human society than freedom. But seest Thou these stones in this parched and barren wilderness? Turn them into bread, and mankind will run after Thee like a flock of sheep, grateful and obedient, though forever trembling, lest Thou withdraw Thy hand and deny them Thy bread." But Thou wouldst not deprive man of freedom and didst reject the offer, thinking, what is that freedom worth, if obedience is bought with bread? Thou didst reply that man lives not by bread alone. But dost Thou know that for the sake of that earthly bread the spirit of the earth will rise up against Thee and will strive with Thee and overcome Thee, and all will follow him, crying, "Who can compare with this beast? He has given us fire from heaven!" Dost Thou know that the ages will pass, and humanity will proclaim by the lips of their sages that there is no crime, and therefore no sin; there is only hunger? "Feed men, and then ask of them virtue!" that's what they'll write on the banner which they will raise against Thee, and with which they will destroy Thy temple. Where Thy temple stood will rise a new building; the terrible tower of Babel will be built again, and though, like the one of old, it will not be finished, yet Thou mightest have prevented that new tower and have cut short the sufferings of men for a thousand years; for they will come back to us after a thousand years of agony with their tower. They will seek us again, hidden underground in the catacombs, for we shall be again persecuted and tortured. They will find us and cry to us, "Feed us, for those who have promised us fire from heaven haven't given it!" And then we shall finish building their tower, for he finishes the building who feeds them. And we alone shall feed them in Thy name, declaring falsely that it is in Thy name. Oh, never, never can they feed themselves without us! No science will give them bread so long as they remain free. In the end they will lay their freedom at our feet, and say to us, "Make us your slaves, but feed us." They will understand themselves, at last, that freedom and bread enough for all are inconceivable together, for never, never will they be able to share between them! They will be convinced, too, that they can never be free, for they are weak, vicious, worthless and rebellious. Thou didst promise them the bread of Heaven, but, I repeat again, can it compare with earthly bread in the eyes of the weak, ever-sinful and ignoble race of man? And if for the sake of the bread of Heaven thousands and tens of thousands shall follow Thee, what is to become of the millions and tens of thousands of millions of creatures who will not have the strength to forego the earthly bread for the sake of the heavenly? Or dost Thou care only for the tens of thousands of the great and strong, while the millions, numerous as the sands of the sea, who are weak but love Thee, must exist only for the sake of the great and strong? No, we care for the weak, too. They are sinful and rebellious, but in the end they too will become obedient. They will marvel at us and look on us as gods, because we are ready to endure the freedom which they have found so dreadful and to rule over them—so awful it will seem to them to be free. But we shall tell them that we are Thy servants and rule them in Thy name. We shall deceive them again, for we will not let Thee come to us again. That deception will be our suffering, for we shall be forced to lie.

" 'This is the significance of the first question in the wilderness, and this is what Thou hast rejected for the sake of that freedom which Thou hast exalted above everything. Yet in this question lies hidden the great secret of this world. Choosing "bread," Thou wouldst have satisfied the universal and everlasting craving of humanity—to find someone to worship. So long as man remains free he strives for nothing so incessantly and so painfully as to find someone to worship. But man seeks to worship what is established beyond dispute, so that all men would agree at once to worship it. For these pitiful creatures are concerned not only to find what one or the other can worship, but to find something that all would believe in and worship; what is essential is that all may be *together* in it. This craving for *community* of worship is the chief misery of every man individually and of all humanity from the beginning of time. For the sake of common worship they've slain each other with the sword. They have set up gods and challenged one another, "Put away your gods and come and worship ours, or we will kill you and your gods!" And so it will be to the end of the world, even when gods disappear from the earth; they will fall down before idols just the same. Thou didst know, Thou couldst not but have known, this fundamental secret of human nature, but Thou didst reject the one infallible banner which was offered Thee to make all men bow down to Thee alone —the banner of earthly bread; and Thou hast rejected it for the sake of freedom and the bread of Heaven. Behold what Thou didst further. And all again in the name of freedom! I tell Thee that man is tormented by no greater anxiety than to find someone quickly to whom he can hand over the gift of freedom with which the ill-fated creature is born. But only one who can appease their conscience can take over their freedom. In bread there was offered Thee an invincible banner; give bread, and man will worship Thee, for nothing is more certain than bread. But if someone else gains possession of his conscience—oh! then he will cast away Thy bread and follow after him who has ensnared his conscience. In that Thou wast right. For the secret of man's being is not only to live but to have something to live for. Without a stable conception of the object of life, man would not consent to go on living, and would rather destroy himself than remain on earth, though he had bread in abundance. That is true. But what happened? Instead of taking men's freedom from them, Thou didst make it greater than ever! Didst Thou forget that man prefers peace, and even death, to freedom of choice in the knowledge of good and evil? Nothing is more seductive for man than his freedom of conscience, but nothing is a greater cause of suffering. And behold, instead of giving a firm foundation for setting the conscience of man at rest forever, Thou didst choose all that is exceptional, vague and enigmatic; Thou didst choose what was utterly beyond the strength of men, acting as though Thou didst not love them at all—Thou who didst come to give Thy life for them! Instead of taking possession of man's freedom, Thou didst increase it, and burdened the spiritual kingdom of mankind with its sufferings forever. Thou didst desire man's free love, that he should follow Thee freely, enticed and taken captive by Thee. In place of the rigid, ancient law, man must hereafter with free heart decide for himself what is good and what is evil, having only Thy image before him as his guide. But didst Thou not know he would at last reject even Thy image and Thy truth, if he is weighed down with the fearful burden of free choice? They will cry aloud at last that the truth is not in Thee, for they could not have been left in greater confusion and suffering than Thou hast caused, laying upon them so many cares and unanswerable problems.

" 'So that, in truth, Thou didst Thyself lay the foundation for the destruction of Thy kingdom, and no one is more to blame for it. Yet what was offered Thee? There are three powers, three powers alone, able to conquer and to hold captive forever the conscience of these impotent rebels for their happiness—those forces are miracle, mystery and authority. Thou hast rejected all three and hast set the example for doing so. When the wise and dread spirit set Thee on the pinnacle of the temple and said to Thee, "If Thou wouldst know whether Thou art the Son of God then cast Thyself down, for it is written: the angels shall hold him up lest he fall and bruise himself, and Thou shalt know then whether Thou art the Son of God and shalt prove then how great is Thy faith in Thy Father." But Thou didst refuse and wouldst not cast Thyself down. Oh! of course, Thou didst proudly and well like God; but the weak, unruly race of men, are they gods? Oh, Thou didst know then that in taking one step, in making one movement to cast Thyself down, Thou wouldst be tempting God and have lost all Thy faith in Him, and wouldst have been dashed to pieces against that earth which Thou didst come to save. And the wise spirit that tempted Thee would have rejoiced. But I ask again, are there many like Thee? And couldst Thou believe for one moment that men, too, could face such a temptation? Is the nature of men such that they can reject miracle, and at the great moments of their life, the moments of their deepest, most agonizing spiritual difficulties, cling only to the free verdict of the heart? Oh, Thou didst know that Thy deed would be recorded in books, would be handed down to remote times and the utmost ends of the earth, and Thou didst hope that man, following Thee, would cling to God and not ask for a miracle. But Thou didst not know that when man rejects miracle he rejects God too; for man seeks not so much God as the miraculous. And as man cannot bear to be without the miraculous, he will create new miracles of his own for himself, and will worship deeds of sorcery and witchcraft, though he might be a hundred times over a rebel, heretic and infidel. Thou didst not come down from the Cross when they shouted to Thee, mocking and reviling Thee, "Come down from the Cross and we will believe that Thou art He." Thou didst not come down, for again Thou wouldst not enslave man by a miracle, and didst crave faith given freely, not based on miracle. Thou didst crave for free love and not the base raptures of the slave before the might that has overawed him forever. But Thou didst think too highly of men therein, for they are slaves, of course, though rebellious by nature. Look round and judge; fifteen centuries have passed; look upon them. Whom hast Thou raised up to Thyself? I swear, man is weaker and baser by nature than Thou hast believed him! Can he, can he do what Thou didst? By showing him so much respect, Thou didst, as it were, cease to feel for

him, for Thou didst ask far too much from him—Thou
who hast loved him more than Thyself! Respecting him
less, Thou wouldst have asked less of him. That would
have been more like love, for his burden would have
been lighter. He is weak and vile. What though he is
everywhere now rebelling against our power, and proud
of his rebellion? It is the pride of a child and a school-
boy. They are little children rioting and barring out
the teacher at school. But their childish delight will
end; it will cost them dear. They will cast down temples
and drench the earth with blood. But they will see at
last, the foolish children, that, though they are rebels,
they are impotent rebels, unable to keep up their own
rebellion. Bathed in their foolish tears, they will recog-
nize at last that He who created them rebels must have
meant to mock at them. They will say this in despair,
and their utterance will be a blasphemy which will
make them more unhappy still, for man's nature cannot
bear blasphemy, and in the end always avenges it on
itself. And so unrest, confusion and unhappiness—that
is the present lot of man after Thou didst bear so much
for their freedom! Thy great prophet tells in vision and
in image that he saw all those who took part in the first
resurrection and that there were of each tribe twelve
thousand. But if there were so many of them, they must
have been not men but gods. They had borne Thy cross,
they had endured scores of years in the barren, hungry
wilderness, living upon locusts and roots—and Thou
mayest indeed point with pride at those children of freedom, of free love, of free and splendid sacrifice for Thy
name. But remember that they were only some thousands; and what of the rest? And how are the other weak
ones to blame, because they could not endure what the

strong have endured? How is the weak soul to blame that it is unable to receive such terrible gifts? Canst Thou have simply come to the elect and for the elect? But if so, it is a mystery and we cannot understand it. And if it is a mystery, we too have a right to preach a mystery, and to teach them that it's not the free judgment of their hearts, not love, that matters, but a mystery which they must follow blindly, even against their conscience. So we have done. We have corrected Thy work and have founded it upon *miracle, mystery* and *authority.* And men rejoiced that they were again led like sheep, and that the terrible gift that had brought them such suffering was, at last, lifted from their hearts. Were we right teaching them this? Speak! Did we not love mankind, so meekly acknowledging their feebleness, lovingly lightening their burden, and permitting their weak nature even sin with our sanction? Why hast Thou come now to hinder us? And why dost Thou look silently and searchingly at me with Thy mild eyes? Be angry. I don't want Thy love, for I love Thee not. And what use is it for me to hide anything from Thee? Don't I know to Whom I am speaking? All that I can say is known to Thee already. And is it for me to conceal from Thee our mystery? Perhaps it is Thy will to hear it from my lips. Listen, then. We are not working with Thee, but with *him*—that is our mystery. It's long —eight centuries—since we have been on *his* side and not on Thine. Just eight centuries ago, we took from him what Thou didst reject with scorn, that last gift he offered Thee, showing Thee all the kingdoms of the earth. We took from him Rome and the sword of Cæsar, and proclaimed ourselves sole rulers of the earth, though hitherto we have not been able to complete our work.

But whose fault is that? Oh, the work is only beginning, but it has begun. It has long to await completion and the earth has yet much to suffer, but we shall triumph and shall be Cæsars, and then we shall plan the universal happiness of man. But Thou mightest have taken even the sword of Cæsar. Why didst Thou reject that last gift? Hadst Thou accepted that last counsel of the mighty spirit, Thou wouldst have accomplished all that man seeks on earth—that is, someone to worship, someone to keep his conscience, and some means of uniting all in one unanimous and harmonious ant heap, for the craving for universal unity is the third and last anguish of men. Mankind as a whole has always striven to organize a universal state. There have been many great nations with great histories, but the more highly they were developed the more unhappy they were, for they felt more acutely than other people the craving for world-wide union. The great conquerors, Timours and Genghis Khans, whirled like hurricanes over the face of the earth, striving to subdue its people, and they too were but the unconscious expression of the same craving for universal unity. Hadst Thou taken the world and Cæsar's purple, Thou wouldst have founded the universal state and have given universal peace. For who can rule men if not he who holds their conscience and their bread in his hands? We have taken the sword of Cæsar, and in taking it, of course, have rejected Thee and followed *him*. Oh, ages are yet to come of the confusion of free thought, of their science and cannibalism. For having begun to build their tower of Babel without us, they will end, of course, with cannibalism. But then the beast will crawl to us and lick our feet and spatter them with tears of blood. And we shall sit upon the beast and raise the cup, and on it will be written, "Mystery." But then, and only then, the reign of peace and happiness will come for men. Thou art proud of Thine elect, but Thou hast only the elect, while we give rest to all. And besides, how many of those elect, those mighty ones who could become elect, have grown weary waiting for Thee, and have transferred and will transfer the powers of their spirit and the warmth of their heart to the other camp, and end by raising their *free* banner against Thee. Thou didst Thyself lift up that banner. But with us all will be happy and will no more rebel, nor destroy one another as under Thy freedom. Oh, we shall persuade them that they will only become free when they renounce their freedom to us and submit to us. And shall we be right or shall we be lying? They will be convinced that we are right, for they will remember the horrors of slavery and confusion to which Thy freedom brought them. Freedom, free thought and science, will lead them into such straits and will bring them face to face with such marvels and insoluble mysteries that some of them, the fierce and rebellious, will destroy themselves; others, rebellious but weak, will destroy one another, while the rest, weak and unhappy, will crawl fawning to our feet and whine to us: "Yes, you were right, you alone possess His mystery, and we come back to you, save us from ourselves!"

" 'Receiving bread from us, they will see clearly that we take the bread made by their hands from them, to give it to them, without any miracle. They will see that we do not change the stones to bread, but in truth they will be more thankful for taking it from our hands than for the bread itself! For they will remember only too well that in old days, without our help, even the bread they made turned to stones in their hands, while since they have come back to us, the very stones have turned to bread in their hands. Too, too well they know the value of complete submission! And until men know that, they will be unhappy. Who is most to blame for their not knowing it, speak? Who scattered the flock and sent it astray on unknown paths? But the flock will come together again and will submit once more, and then it will be once for all. Then we shall give them the quiet humble happiness of weak creatures such as they are by nature. Oh, we shall persuade them at last not to be proud, for Thou didst lift them up and thereby taught them to be proud. We shall show them that they are weak, that they are only pitiful children, but that child-like happiness is the sweetest of all. They will become timid and will look to us and huddle close to us in fear, as chicks to the hen. They will marvel at us and will be awe-stricken before us, and will be proud at our being so powerful and clever, that we have been able to sub-due such a turbulent flock of thousands of millions. They will tremble impotently before our wrath, their minds will grow fearful, they will be quick to shed tears like women and children, but they will be just as ready at a sign from us to pass to laughter and rejoicing, to happy mirth and childish song. Yes, we shall set them to work, but in their leisure hours we shall make their life like a child's game, with children's songs and inno-cent dance. Oh, we shall allow them even sin; they are weak and helpless, and they will love us like children because we allow them to sin. We shall tell them that every sin will be expiated, if it is done with our per-mission, that we allow them to sin because we love them, and the punishment for these sins we take upon ourselves. And we shall take it upon ourselves, and they will adore us as their saviors who have taken on themselves their sins before God. And they will have no secrets from us. We shall allow or forbid them to live with their wives and mistresses, to have or not to have children—according to whether they have been obedient or disobedient—and they will submit to us gladly and cheerfully. The most painful secrets of their conscience, all, all they will bring to us, and we shall have an answer for all. And they will be glad to believe our answer, for it will save them from the great anxiety and terrible agony they endure at present in making a free decision for themselves. And all will be happy, all the millions of creatures, except the hundred thousand who rule over them. For only we, we who guard the mystery, shall be unhappy. There will be thousands of millions of happy babes, and a hundred thousand sufferers who have taken upon themselves the curse of the knowledge of good and evil. Peacefully they will die, peacefully they will expire in Thy name, and beyond the grave they will find nothing but death. But we shall keep the secret, and for their happiness we shall allure them with the reward of heaven and eternity. Though if there were anything in the other world, it certainly would not be for such as they. It is prophesied that Thou wilt come again in victory, Thou wilt come with Thy chosen, the proud and strong, but we will say that they have only saved themselves, but we have saved all. We are told that the harlot who sits upon the beast, and holds in her hands the *mystery,* shall be put to shame, that the weak will rise up again, and will rend her royal purple and will strip naked her loathsome body. But then I will stand up and point out to Thee the thousand mil-

lions of happy children who have known no sin. And
we who have taken their sins upon us for their happiness will stand up before Thee and say: "Judge us if
Thou canst and darest." Know that I fear Thee not.
Know that I too have been in the wilderness, I too have
lived on roots and locusts, I too prized the freedom with
which Thou hast blessed men, and I too was striving to
stand among Thy elect, among the strong and powerful,
thirsting "to make up the number." But I awakened and
would not serve madness. I turned back and joined the
ranks of those *who have corrected Thy work.* I left
the proud and went back to the humble, for the happiness of the humble. What I say to Thee will come to
pass, and our dominion will be built up. I repeat, tomorrow Thou shalt see that obedient flock who at a
sign from me will hasten to heap up the hot cinders
about the pile on which I shall burn Thee for coming
to hinder us. For if anyone has ever deserved our fires,
it is Thou. Tomorrow I shall burn Thee. *Dixi.*'"

Ivan stopped. He was carried away as he talked and
spoke with excitement; when he had finished, he suddenly smiled.

Alyosha had listened in silence; toward the end he
was greatly moved and seemed several times on the point
of interrupting, but restrained himself. Now his words
came with a rush.

"But . . . that's absurd!" he cried, flushing. "Your
poem is in praise of Jesus, not in blame of Him—as you
meant it to be. And who will believe you about freedom? Is that the way to understand it? That's not the
idea of it in the Orthodox Church . . . That's Rome,
and not even the whole of Rome, it's false—those are
the worst of the Catholics, the Inquisitors, the Jesuits!

. . . And there could not be such a fantastic creature as your Inquisitor. What are these sins of mankind they take on themselves? Who are these keepers of the mystery who have taken some curse upon themselves for the happiness of mankind? When have they been seen? We know the Jesuits, they are spoken ill of, but surely they are not what you describe? They are not that at all, not at all. . . . They are simply the Romish army for the earthly sovereignty of the world in the future, with the Pontiff of Rome for Emperor . . . that's their ideal, but there's no sort of mystery or lofty melancholy about it. . . . It's simple lust of power, of filthy earthly gain, of domination—something like a universal serfdom with them as masters—that's all they stand for. They don't even believe in God, perhaps. Your suffering inquisitor is a mere fantasy."

"Stay, stay," laughed Ivan, "how hot you are! A fantasy you say, let it be so! Of course it's a fantasy. But allow me to say: do you really think that the Roman Catholic movement of the last centuries is actually nothing but the lust of power, of filthy earthly gain? Is that Father Païssy's teaching?"

"No, no, on the contrary, Father Païssy did once say something the same as you . . . but of course it's not the same, not a bit the same," Alyosha hastily corrected himself.

"A precious admission, in spite of your 'not a bit the same.' I ask you why your Jesuits and inquisitors have united simply for vile material gain? Why can there not be among them one martyr oppressed by great sorrow and loving humanity? You see, only suppose that there was one such man among all those who desire nothing but filthy material gain—if there's only one like my old inquisitor, who had himself eaten roots in the desert and made frenzied efforts to subdue his flesh to make himself free and perfect. But yet all his life he loved humanity, and suddenly his eyes were opened, and he saw that it is no great moral blessedness to attain per- fection and freedom, if at the same time one gains the conviction that billions of God's creatures have been created as a mockery, that they will never be capable of using their freedom, that these poor rebels can never turn into giants to complete the tower, that it was not for such geese that the great idealist dreamt his dream of harmony. Seeing all that, he turned back and joined —the clever people. Surely that could have happened?"

"Joined whom, what clever people?" cried Alyosha, completely carried away. "They have no such great cleverness and no mysteries and secrets. . . . Perhaps nothing but atheism, that's all their secret. Your in- quisitor does not believe in God, that's his secret!"

"What if it is so! At last you have guessed it. It's per- fectly true that that's the whole secret, but isn't that suffering, at least for a man like that, who has wasted his whole life in the desert and yet could not shake off his incurable love of humanity? In his old age he reached the clear conviction that nothing but the advice of the great dread spirit could build up any tolerable sort of life for the feeble, unruly, 'incomplete, empirical creatures created in jest.' And so, convinced of this, he sees that he must follow the council of the wise spirit, the dread spirit of death and destruction, and therefore accept lying and deception, and lead men consciously to death and destruction, and yet deceive them all the way so that they may not notice where they are being led, that the poor, blind creatures may at least on the way think themselves happy. And note, the deception is in the name of Him in Whose ideal the old man had so fervently believed all his life long. Is not that tragic? And if only one such stood at the head of the whole army 'filled with the lust of power only for the sake of filthy gain'—would not one such be enough to make a tragedy? More than that, one such standing at the head is enough to create the actual leading idea of the Roman Church with all its armies and Jesuits, its highest idea. I tell you frankly that I firmly believe that there has always been such a man among those who stood at the head of the movement. Who knows, there may have been some such even among the Roman Popes. Who knows, perhaps the spirit of that accursed old man who loves mankind so obstinately in his own way is to be found even now in a whole multitude of such old men, existing not by chance but by agreement, as a secret league formed long ago for the guarding of the mystery, to guard it from the weak and the unhappy, so as to make them happy. No doubt it is so, and so it must be indeed. I fancy that even among the Masons there's something of the same mystery at the bottom, and that that's why the Catholics so detest the Masons as their rivals breaking up the unity of the idea, while it is so essential that there should be one flock and one shepherd. . . . But from the way I defend my idea I might be an author impatient of your criticism. Enough of it."

"You are perhaps a Mason yourself!" broke suddenly from Alyosha. "You don't believe in God," he added, speaking this time very sorrowfully. He fancied besides that his brother was looking at him ironically. "How does your poem end?" he asked, suddenly looking down. "Or was it the end?"

"I meant it to end like this: When the Inquisitor ceased speaking, he waited some time for his Prisoner to answer him. His silence weighed down upon him. He saw the Prisoner had listened intently all the time, looking gently in his face and evidently not wishing to reply. The old man longed for Him to say something, however bitter and terrible. But He suddenly approached the old man in silence and softly kissed him on his bloodless, aged lips. That was all his answer. The old man shuddered. His lips moved. He went to the door, opened it, and said to him: 'Go, and come no more. . . . Come not at all, never, never!' And he let him out into the dark alleys of the town. The Prisoner went away."

"And the old man?"

"The kiss glows in his heart, but the old man adheres to his idea."

"And you with him, you too?" cried Alyosha, mournfully.

Ivan laughed.

"Why, it's all nonsense, Alyosha. It's only a senseless poem of a senseless student, who could never write two lines of verse. Why do you take it so seriously? Surely you don't suppose I am going straight off to the Jesuits, to join the men who are correcting His work? Good Lord, it's no business of mine. I told you, all I want is to live on to thirty, and then . . . dash the cup to the ground!"

"But the little sticky leaves, and the precious tombs, and the blue sky, and the woman you love! How will you live, how will you love them?" Alyosha cried sorrowfully. "With such a hell in your heart and your head, how can you? No, that's just what you are going away for, to join them . . . if not, you will kill yourself, you can't endure it!"

"There is a strength to endure everything," Ivan said with a cold smile.

"What strength?"

"The strength of the Karamazovs—the strength of the Karamazov baseness."

"To sink into debauchery, to stifle your soul with corruption, yes?"

"Possibly even that . . . only perhaps till I am thirty I shall escape it, and then—"

"How will you escape it? By what will you escape it? That's impossible with your ideas."

"In the Karamazov way, again."

" 'Everything is lawful,' you mean? Everything is lawful, is that it?"

Ivan scowled, and all at once turned strangely pale.

"Ah, you've caught up yesterday's phrase, which so offended Miüsov—and which Dmitri pounced upon so naïvely and paraphrased!" he smiled queerly. "Yes, if you like, 'everything is lawful' since the word has been said. I won't deny it. And Mitya's version isn't bad."

Alyosha looked at him in silence.

"I thought that going away from here I have you at least," Ivan said suddenly, with unexpected feeling; "but now I see that there is no place for me even in your heart, my dear hermit. The formula, 'all is lawful,' I won't renounce—will you renounce me for that, yes?"

Alyosha got up, went to him and softly kissed him on the lips.

"That's plagiarism," cried Ivan, highly delighted.

"You stole that from my poem. Thank you, though. Get up, Alyosha, it's time we were going, both of us."

They went out, but stopped when they reached the entrance of the restaurant.

"Listen, Alyosha," Ivan began in a resolute voice, "if I am really able to care for the sticky little leaves, I shall only love them remembering you. It's enough for me that you are somewhere here, and I shan't lose my desire for life yet. Is that enough for you? Take it as a declaration of love if you like. And now you go to the right and I to the left. And it's enough, do you hear— enough! I mean even if I don't go away tomorrow (I think I certainly shall go) and we meet again, don't say a word more on these subjects. I beg that particularly. And about Dmitri, too, I ask you especially never speak to me again," he added, with sudden irritation; "it's all exhausted, it has all been said over and over again, hasn't it? And I'll make you one promise in return for it. When, at thirty, I want to 'dash the cup to the ground,' wherever I may be I'll come to have one more talk with you, even though it were from America—you may be sure of that. I'll come on purpose. It will be very interesting to have a look at you, to see what you'll be by that time. It's rather a solemn promise, you see. And we really may be parting for seven years or ten. Come, go now to your Pater Seraphicus, he is dying. If he dies without you, you will be angry with me for having kept you. Good-bye, kiss me once more; that's right, now go."